What the Eye Sees

Alan Maley

First published in 2018 by Plain Words Press
13 Water Meadows
Fordwich
Kent
CT2 0BF
UK

Copyright @ 2018 Alan Maley
ISBN 978-1-905171-01-9

Cover photograph. Chrysa Papalazarou
Drawings: Andrew Wright.

Printed in Great Britain by D.Isom Printers, Herne Bay, UK.

ii

Acknowledgements.

I am grateful to David Cobb for introducing me to haiku and to the British Haiku Society for sustaining my interest since its foundation in 1990.

Many friends have helped by reading and offering constructive feedback over the years, for which I am most grateful: Michael Swan, Alan Duff, David Hill, Viviane Dunn, Malu Sciamarelli, Andrew Wright, Jane Spiro, Patrick Early.

I have learned a lot from working on creative writing courses with my students in Singapore and Bangkok in the 1990's. The stimulus of working with the members of the Asian Teacher-Writer Group from 2003-14 was also invaluable to my continuing interest in writing haiku.

I am especially grateful to Andrew Wright for his beautiful illustrations and to Chrysa Papalazarou for the striking cover photograph.

Introduction

What the Eye Sees is the first of three volumes of haiku selected from the thousands I have written over the past 20 years or so. The other two volumes, *How the Heart Responds* and *Where the Wind Blows* are available in the same series.

Many people are now familiar with the haiku form in English but for those who are not, here is a brief introduction.

The haiku is a verse form which developed in Japan in the 17th century. Essentially, haiku aim to sharpen our observation and perception of the world around us, especially of natural phenomena. The haiku is like a snapshot of a moment of heightened awareness – what some western writers call an epiphany. So the starting point in writing a haiku is the recognition of this special 'haiku moment'. This may be, and often is, the observation of something 'ordinary', which we would otherwise take for granted – a frog jumping into a pond, cold leeks being washed, a farmer ploughing followed by seagulls... What the haiku is supposed to do is to transform these ordinary phenomena into a moment of enhanced appreciation and to spark reflection about the way the world is.

In traditional Japanese haiku there are quite a number of rules. For example, the rules prescribe a text of 17 syllables (not words) arranged in three lines of 5, 7 and 5 syllables respectively. The haiku should have a season word which sets the moment in a specific time of year. Haikus are not expected to rhyme, though they do make extensive use of internal rhyme, alliteration and assonance. The language aims for simplicity and precision, avoiding self-conscious literary tropes, like metaphor, and high-sounding vocabulary. Usually, the first two lines set the scene by offering a sharp image of the haiku moment. The third line then shocks the reader into a new way of perceiving that moment.

Western interest in the haiku form developed in the 20th century, especially in the UK and the USA, stimulated by the pioneer work of R. H. Blyth and experimental poets, like Ezra Pound in the 1920's and 30's. The Beat Generation, led by Jack Kerouac and Gary Snyder, also found the haiku a congenial form of expression. There is also a strong connection between haiku and Zen Buddhist practice.

As is normal when cultural borrowing takes place, the original Japanese form has been to some degree transmuted in its transfer to English. Many writers of haiku no longer subscribe to the 5-7-5 rule, for example, claiming that it does not sit comfortably with the structure of western languages. This results in free-form haiku of varying syllabic length, though usually the 3 line structure is preserved. There are even, however examples of one-line haikus.

In this collection, I have stuck mainly to the traditional 5-7-5 structure. This is largely because I find the formal constraints it imposes actually stimulate inventiveness and creative energy – what the T'ang poet describes as 'dancing in chains'.

For me, writing haiku has become a daily practice. It helps me feel more alive and more in tune with the natural world. It is both a form of mental hygiene and a creative resource.

In this book, *What the Eye Sees*, I have tried, with varying degrees of success, to select haikus which come as close as possible to the ideal of stating simply what is observed with a minimum of intervention and comment by the writer. I have grouped the haiku into three sections: *Nature, Birds* and *Seasons* but this is purely for convenience and there is clearly quite a lot of overlap between sections.

I hope readers will enjoy at least some of the following haiku and perhaps acquire a taste for writing some of their own. One way of finding out more about haiku is to access the website of The British Haiku Society (BHS) **www.britishhaikusociety.org.uk** *The Genius of Haiku: Readings from R. H. Blyth* is another very useful resource.

Nature

this red butterfly
rests on a leaf, wings folded –
a prey in waiting

the sun smouldering
in the ashes of evening:
wind fans the embers...

snow, blurring the grass,
freaking the hedgerow's bleak sticks,
whiskering the dog

the bamboo bent low
under the weight of wet leaves –
so heavy the rain…

these last blackberries,
drugged by late September sun:
innocent of frost

this tractor dawdles –
a flock of seagulls behind –
pickering the spoils

wild garlic, nettles,
laced together with goose grass –
a flirt of wings

a breath in the woods
stirs the leaves before they fall.
brief rustling – silence

dark by half past four:
stopping on this marshland path,
the slow drip of leaves

outside my window
the old vine rustles its leaves –
grapes hollowed by wasps

after the day's heat,
this feather dust of night rain –
leaves put out their tongues

mist and wood smoke rise,
lit from behind by dying
daylight - now the moon...

after the rain, mist.
now the valley fills with milk,
curdling the air

these last white roses,
high on winter spindle stems
- every day, fewer

cold rain, dark bleak mud,
yet on these twigs of blackthorn.
the first green budding

first horse-chestnut leaves,
wing struts folded like green bats,
waiting for evening

a mist of bluebells
floats inches above the ground
in the springtime wood

air thick with honey
as blackthorn blossom explodes –
we forget the thorns

the woods are a wall,
dark against the bright green fields –
a sudden shudder…

beech trees rattle coins
in the pocket of the wind –
soon to scatter them

on this plantain leaf
shadow puppets flicker
as wind stirs the trees

I learn to read trees -
the lexis of leaves, the forked
syntax of branches

a hump-backed whale cloud
basks in the morning sunlight
filling the valley

this morning silence,
as crystal cool as the air –
now a distant bell

how did Turner know
when he painted tonight's sky
it would be like this?

dead tree trunks erect,
roots now deep under water –
leaves a distant memory

dead tree
arms outstretched
crucified on the sky

old arthritic trees
branches twisted out of true
yet this spurt of leaves

frost on an oak leaf –
patterns of silver pinheads
nailed tight together

a single white birch
stands out in the dark woodland
this winter morning

these moss-quilted stones,
a cascade of ruined barns –
fossil smells of sheep

trees know what to do:
when to bud, when to drop leaves –
a good example...

frost on bamboo leaves,
silvering over the green,
sharpening the blades

the leaf twirls downwards
aiming for its reflection –
a perfect touchdown

after weeks of drought
this featherdust of dawn rain –
I smell the earth breathe

even these low hills
are high enough for those who've
never seen the Alps

the last leaf hanging
by a toenail to the branch –
a puff of wind, and...

in the old reed beds
a green fire of this year's growth
smouldering outwards

this first dragonfly –
its amber wings shimmering,
embalmed in sunshine

deep down underground
worms blind-taste the falling rain,
relish the cool earth

one October bee
clinging on for dear life
to a fuchsia bell

arthritic marsh trees
sculpted by relentless wind –
beauty at a price

last year's blackberries,
now perfectly mummified –
my palate tingles

day grey as wet steel,
wind sharp as a meat cleaver –
sudden goldfinches

darkness visible
as black water sleeps at dusk –
not a whiff of wind

a looming presence,
this gigantic carp, lurking,
lips pouting, ready…

I feel the rough rasp
of the sandstone window ledge –
still warm at evening

woods wadded by snow,
quilted with quiet darkness –
the cold creak of boots

in the lane outside
the first rustle of dead leaves –
a shiver of wind

the sky is a bruise –
jaundiced around the edges,
plum-black at its heart

all these miles inland
the end of the tide's tether –
this last salt ripple

river, treacle dark,
in slow spate after May rains,
heaves heavy downstream

sullen pewter sea –
Oshima draped in dawn mist –
sudden glint of sun

the throat of a wave,
emerald under pearl froth –
hold your breath – it's break…

molasses river,
rum dark, thick with sediment,
treacling to the sea

hushed catspaws of wind,
the soft sobbing of the rain –
a shutter rattles

walking with the dog,
blackberries bruised by autumn –
wind across the lakes

Birds

the sky's blue blanket,
blown inside out by spring squalls –
starbursts of seagulls

Persil-white swans moored
in midstream – their necks posing
elegant questions

this slate-grey heron
stands hunched in lakeside sedges...
spear at the ready

two geese ~ pink-bellied
slowly saw the sky in half –
shadows on the snow

sudden kingfisher
unzips the afternoon air
above the river

the stiff grey heron
cranks himself off the river –
defies gravity

swan flying through snow:
white on white – navigating
blind, seeking the lake

winter ducks huddle
in the lee of a reed brake –
bobbing on the waves

gulls graze the surface –
leave a trail of crystal drops
then flick into air

magpie in the tree,
using your tail to balance –
hop – the branch springs back

cormorants, heavy
with wet, black feathers, trundle
across the surface

the swallows are back,
stitching the air on the lake
in elegant loops...

the gull soars, plummets -
a nick in the lake's surface,
then he soars again

the owls' double flute
in their last dawn foraging –
greying into day

stonechats chipping air
into sharp splinters of sound
this perfect morning

over the snow fields
and the black sticks of the woods
flocks of winter gulls

on the cusp of dawn
this owl flies on wadded wings
sweeping up the dark

late afternoon dark –
I hear gulls above the lake
just out of eyeshot

a fleet of seagulls
skirmish at anchor, icebound,
waiting for orders

these gulls, skirmishing.
slim pickings from the river –
the lake frozen hard

on the frozen lake
sun lays down a blinding path –
two swans ice-breaking

frost-chilled swan, so white –
I think of Basho's cold leeks
washed white in winter

gulls in random flight
punctuating the grey sky
but making no sense

winter furrowed field –
a scatter of gulls settle –
snowflakes in the wind

long-tailed tits hover –
puppets suspended in air –
but no strings attached

a pair of herons
gliding in a slow circle –
a Japanese screen

swans doing yoga –
heads down, tails up – concentrate –
now you can relax...

two swans arch their necks,
interrogating the river –
dredging up secrets

white snow and black crow:
hard white pellets bouncing off
black lacquer feathers

the kestrel hovers
above the looking-glass lake –
spears his reflection

bamboo under snow,
leaves piled high with it, until
this sudden sparrow...

the plump sultana
in the blackbird's yellow beak: –
suddenly, it's gone

by the riverbank,
a draggle of wet feathers –
a swan slowly rots

grey geese on green grass
outside the abbey ruins –
untroubled by god

tentative swallows
criss-crossing the evening sky,
taking their bearings

guttural pheasants
crawking from the undergrowth –
how do they survive?

sunlight on the lake,
making a pewter mirror...
and one silent swan

this summer evening,
in the cathedral of trees –
vespers sung by birds...

a pair of plump geese
querulous on the lake shore
fly off, still squabbling

Seasons

Winter

figs in February,
fossils unripe on the bough –
who will eat them now?

rhododendron buds
tightly clenched against the frost
dreaming of spring sun

a poultice of leaves
covers winter woodland wounds,
healing toward spring

December hazels,
the last leaves barely fallen –
these sudden catkins

mid-December day,
the sun's brightness brings no heat:
a brittle, sham smile

plum-dark clouds looming
through the lace of winter trees –
first, fat drops spatter...

winter daffodils
will live to regret these blooms
when the frost returns

a sudden snow shower
pricking the lake with pin-points –
in bright sunshine

there's snow in the air.
I can smell it, all the way
from the Russian steppes...

sun-brushed winter woods –
silver tuning forks, waiting
for wind to strike them

scrubbing winter beet
in an old bathtub outside –
first I break the ice

bone-cold, black water
gilded with winter sunshine –
the first rays of hope

on the path, slide marks
where the unwary have slipped –
now frozen solid

secondary storms
as wind whips snow off branches,
powdering crows' wings

crystalline patterns
on childhood winter windows –
my breath a thick fog

deep beneath the snow
beyond the reach of frostbite
worms plot their comeback

in my crystal ball
I sit, snow swirling round me –
someone's shaken it...
now I'm snow-blinded by it,
lost amidst the storm of white

my boots crunch the snow,
layers of ice underneath –
my old bones so wary...

frayed cords of snow fall –
garden a Japanese screen.
snow pellets sting me

this gun-metal ice
seals the surface of the lake
reflecting the sky

moss, electric green,
caught by slanting winter sun
on the crumbling wall

Spring

a grey day in May –
only the seagulls' shrill cries,
wind flirting the lake

the slow burn of spring
burnishing willow tresses
to bronze in sunlight

spring shedding blossom,
a blizzard of white petals
drifting in pathways

dead willow catkins
littering the grass: April's
votive offerings

thanks be
for treefulness in April
bud-bursting energy

moist, misty April,
morning skeins snagging the woods,
the sun, a red glow

beech-bud cartridges,
tightly wrapped, waiting for spring
to ignite the fuse

bishops' croziers
coiled tight as watch springs –
these ferns in waiting

nettles are wilting
this weary May afternoon –
heads drooping, limp flags

was it just last year
when the buds opened like this?
how could I forget?

April bumblebees
stumbling from flower to flower –
just getting started

all of a sudden
leaves have invaded the paths –
they brush my face now...

this twig-twitching spring,
all chirping and twittering
towards the egg time

spring sycamore buds
sticky brown sweets on twig ends –
just a hint of green

early morning birds
have started to sing again –
don't count your chickens!

Summer

brazen buttercups:
the air heavy with honey –
summer's here at last

late honeysuckle
entwining leafless branches:
summer's dying breath

premonitory:
a single yellow leaf falls –
it's Midsummer's Day

Late summer sequence:

after the harvest,
tractor dicing the stubble:
smell of fresh-turned earth

across the wide field
a swarm of gulls skirmishing
for easy pickings

it's high summer
but autumn is in the air
a whiff of regret...

gilded buttercups
basking in lush summer grass –
before haymaking...

lilac spears rusting
as summer thrusts spring aside –
a fading fragrance

this summer evening,
avant-garde music – scherzo
for five lawn-mowers

late August hotel –
baleful windows overlook
the slow, sad river

this first dragonfly –
its amber wings shimmering,
embalmed in sunshine

drifts of summer snow
as willows shed their kapok –
getting up my nose...

air thick with honey
as blackthorn blossom explodes –
we forget the thorns

on the river path
this green seat, glazed with new rain –
mist filters the bells

water-lily pads
lifting their skirts on the lake –
getting the wind up

Autumn

November sun slants –
my shadow, ten times my length,
stalks me on my walk

October sunshine:
after cold winds, autumn rain…
these last dragonflies

these silver birches,
their leaves, small change thrown reckless
to October winds

these late autumn days:
sunlight watering the lawn,
desperate dragonflies

last fat blackberries,
drugged by late September sun:
innocent of frost

November garden –
a flock of leaves flutters down,
golden wings beating

this cool morning air
smells already of autumn –
the leaves don't know yet

last night I swept up –
now wet leaves plaster the stones –
autumn's calling cards

leaves butterfly up
in this sudden autumn squall –
beautiful – and dead

autumn shivering
into winter – willow leaves
splinter in sunlight

fuzzy grey mornings
as October, yawns, stretches
then starts to shiver...

in the galleries
of the woods, cloths of gold hang
threadbare – in tatters

incandescent trees –
as if lit from inside as
autumn sun strikes them

a wet day, and cold –
last leaves clinging to their perch
dreading winter wind

first frost on the lawn.
sun rising through black branches –
birch leaves floating down

no sooner leaves fall
than buds swell on bare branches –
impatient for spring...

fig leaves turning brown
below my window – autumn –
the fruit still unripe

splintered walnut skulls
spilling their brains on the road –
autumn's wanton waste